Enchanting
VIETNAM

DAVID BOWDEN

JOHN BEAUFOY PUBLISHING

Contents

Above: Cao Dai temples, such as this one in My Tho on the Mekong Delta, are common around Ho Chi Minh City.

Above centre: The French colonial style of architecture is apparent in the Ho Chi Minh City Hall.

Above left: Limestone topography of rounded islands with steep cliffs is a feature of Halong Bay.

Opposite: Buddhist temples, such as Ho Chi Minh City's Thien Hau Pagoda, are where devotees make offerings by burning incense.

Title page: Po Nagar Cham Towers near Nha Trang.

Chapter 1: Country of Inspiring Natural Beauty

While Vietnam's recorded history goes back thousands of years, the Vietnam War (referred to by the Vietnamese as the American War) which raged from 1961 to 1975 is what largely features in the minds of many foreigners. Vietnam is now a country at peace with the upwardly mobile younger generation knowing very little of the disastrous years that killed millions, destroyed much of the countryside and slowed the country's economic development for years afterwards. For the majority of the population, the war years are behind them and most Vietnamese strive for greater economic prosperity. Motorbikes rule the streets of the large cities and are indicative of just how rapidly things are changing in Vietnam.

An estimated population of just over 90 million makes it the world's 13th most populous nation. Most people are ethnic Vietnamese but some 20 per cent are ethnic Chinese, Khmers, Chams or one of 54 ethno-linguistic groups collectively known as hill tribe people. While Vietnam is nominally a Buddhist nation, many religions provide spiritual guidance to the inhabitants.

Known officially as the Socialist Republic of Vietnam, the country has a President as its head and is a single party (the Communist Party of Vietnam) socialist republic with a Prime Minister as head of the government. Hanoi is the capital but Ho Chi Minh City is the largest conurbation and the nation's economic powerhouse. The currency is the *dong* and the official language is Vietnamese.

Vietnamese cuisine, especially its street-food dishes, is well known throughout the world. The most famous dish is beef or chicken *pho* (noodle soup). While Vietnamese food is not as spicy-hot as some other Asian cuisines, chillies are still an important ingredient, though more evident in the food of central and southern Vietnam than in the north. Meats sizzle on charcoal braziers in makeshift roadside stalls all over the country and then there's the locally-grown coffee and *baguettes* laden with tasty treats. In the evening

the *bia hoi* (fresh draught beer) shops spread onto the nation's pavements.

Vietnam's history and natural beauty have inspired many authors, artists and cinematographers – Graham Greene's *The Quiet American* and the French film *Indochine* have helped create the intrigue to lure tourists to visit. What they discover is a lively, vibrant and colourful country with vast cultural diversity and an abundance of natural and leisure-time attractions.

Above and left: Most Vietnamese are Buddhists and temples play an important role in their lives. Smouldering sticks of incense fill the air around temple altars and Buddhist monks seeking alms are a common sight.

Opposite: Ho Chi Minh City's skyline is an eclectic blend of architectural styles from the French-built Hôtel de Ville de Saigon (Ho Chi Minh City Hall) to the ever-rising modern office blocks.

Geography and Climate

Vietnam covers an area of 331,210 km² (128,565 sq miles) and is an elongated country extending 1,145 km (712 miles) north to south between the capital Hanoi and the southern metropolis of Ho Chi Minh City (still referred to by many as Saigon). Its narrowest west-to-east extent is just 50 km (31 miles) in Quang Binh Province. Vietnam extends from 8 to 21° N (making the far north of the country close to the Tropic of Cancer) and 102 to 110° E of Greenwich. Its coastline is 3,444 km (2,140 miles) long and only those places in the far north and north-west are more than 150 km (93 miles) from the coast.

Opposite: The twisting road across the Hai Van Pass north of Danang forms a boundary between the climates of northern and southern Vietnam.

Below: With its long coastline, fishing is an important industry in the country. Many Vietnamese fishermen still use the traditional round bamboo boat called 'thúng chai'.

The country is bordered by China to the north, Laos and Cambodia to the west, the Eastern Sea (South China Sea) along the eastern coastline and the Gulf of Thailand along the south-west coastline.

Vietnam's geography is diverse with a handful of islands including Phu Quoc and Con Dao off the southern coastline as well as long sandy beaches, fertile river plains, pine forests, karst topography and mountainous areas. Forests, mangroves, rice terraces, rounded limestone mountains and vast stretches of beaches and coastal dunes dominate the landscape. Much of Vietnam's natural assets are, however, very altered with only a small percentage of the country unaffected by human activity.

Hills and mountains, such as the Truong Son or Annamite Mountain Range in the centre of the country, make up 75% of the land area. Rivers flow from these mountains, and waterfalls on some are tourist attractions. There are several waterfalls around Da Lat with Prenn Falls to the south of the hill station town being a popular place for tourists to visit.

Vietnam has three distinct regions; north, central and south. Vietnam's two main rivers are the Red River (also known as Song Hong, Song Cai or Mother River) in the north and the Mekong River in the south. The Red River is 1,149 km (714 miles) long and starts in the mountains of Yunnan Province in south-west China before flowing into the sea just south of Haiphong in the Gulf of Tonkin. Its name is derived from the colour of the silt-laden river although, in reality, it is more murky brown than red. The mighty Mekong River enters Vietnam from Cambodia and flows into the Eastern Sea (South China Sea) south of Ho Chi Minh City.

Hanoi is positioned along the Red River while Ho Chi Minh City is on the Saigon River. One of the closest places from HCMC to see the Mekong River is at My Tho on the river delta. The delta is very flat here and is affected by two daily tides. Mud carried down from its source is deposited along the floodplain and its constant renewal is important in the agricultural cycle of the delta.

The country's climate varies and is affected by features

such as proximity to the sea, altitude and latitude. Being a tropical country, Vietnam has a humid, subtropical climate. Temperatures and humidity remain high with the latter averaging 84% for most of the year and for much of the country.

Temperatures reach the high 30s °C (90s °F) during summer with April being the hottest month. However, they can be as low as 5° C (41° F) in the north during winter and the months of December and January especially.

Seasonality is more pronounced in the north. Northern mountains and plateaus have a moderating effect on the tropical climate with the conditions more like those in temperate zones. Seasonal temperature variation in higher altitudes such as around Da Lat and Sapa is less marked and ranges from just 21°C (70°F) to 28°C (82°F) throughout the year. Fireplaces in some resorts in both locations are commonly used in the winter months. Hanoi is a city of extremes – hot in summer and cold in winter.

The tropical weather of central and southern Vietnam

results in luxuriant vegetation and rainforests especially in the central highlands. The seasonal reversal in the movement of tropical air, known as the monsoon, dominates climatic conditions but the effects of rain vary from location to location. Typically, the north-east monsoon from November to April is drier than the south-west monsoon from May to October, which results in heavy rainfall accounting for 90% of the annual precipitation. Between July and November, often violent and unpredictable typhoons can have detrimental effects along the coast from central to north Vietnam. However, when it rains, many Vietnamese simply don a raincoat and get on with their lives.

Above: Much of Vietnam's flat lowlands are farmed. This land in Que Vo, north of Hanoi on the way to Halong Bay, is a mixed farm where vegetables are grown for sale in the capital.

Opposite top: While Prenn Falls south of Da Lat are not high, they are popular with tourists who visit to ride the cable car and walk in the cool forests.

Opposite below: Vietnam's rivers serve many functions: the waters of this one in southern Vietnam on the way to Da Lat are used for both agriculture and fishing.

A Brief History

Throughout its history, Vietnam has been most influenced by India, China, France, Japan and America. The Hindu kingdom of Champa, centred on present-day Danang, flourished from the second to the 15th centuries. Trade with India was active then and ideas, religion and language were borrowed from the subcontinent. Several Champa sites can be visited, the most accessible of which are the Museum of Cham Sculpture in Danang and Nha Trang's ancient Po Nagar brick towers (see page 59).

Various ports in Vietnam, such as Hoi An, one of the best preserved, became important stops along the India to China trade route. Vietnam's independence as a kingdom evolved and various emperors ruled the country until 1945 when the 13th emperor of the Nguyen Dynasty, Bao Dai abdicated.

The French were active in what was known as French Indo-China from 1859 to 1954. Much of the country was controlled by the French with the emperors and local people being reluctantly ruled. Opposition was suppressed by the French but nationalistic feelings were strong and nurtured by the communists as early as 1925. During the Second World War the Japanese left the French administration in place but exploited Vietnam's resources for their own benefit. In 1945, Ho Chi Minh led the Viet Minh Front (communist national independence coalition) during the August Revolution to take control of much of the country and declare its independence.

The French returned and the nationalists took to armed resistance. While the French were finally humiliated in battle at Dien Bien Phu in Vietnam's far north-west, they left a lasting legacy.

The 1954 peace accord with France resulted in the country being divided into two temporary zones at the Ben Hai River (near the 17th parallel). These zones eventually became permanent with the South being anticommunist and the North, communist.

Above: *A statue of Ho Chi Minh outside the Ho Chi Minh City Hall with modern financial buildings in the background.*

Left: The Gallic footprint includes wide boulevards, grand buildings and elements of the cuisine. Less obvious signs of French influence include people wearing berets and the vintage Citroën limousines at the entrance to Hanoi's Hotel Sofitel Legend Metropole.

Below: The infamous 'Hanoi Hilton' was a French-built prison in central Hanoi used to house US airmen shot down over North Vietnam. Known to the French as 'Maison Centrale', now only the gatehouse of Hoa Lo Prison remains and is a museum.

America's involvement officially started in 1961 when military advisers were sent to assist the South Vietnamese in their struggle against the north. During the ensuing war, names and phrases like the Vietcong (or VC), Ho Chi Minh Trail, Khe Sanh, My Lai Massacre, Demilitarized Zone (DMZ) and Tet Offensive were heard regularly by global television audiences.

The war ended on April 30, 1975 with the fall of Saigon. An estimated two million Vietnamese civilians and one million soldiers were killed (American deaths were approximately 60,000), many of the forests were destroyed by the Agent Orange herbicide, and landmines and unexploded ordinances still claim victims each year. More bombs were dropped on Vietnam during the war than on the whole of Europe during the Second World War.

A trade embargo, imposed on Vietnam by the Americans was lifted on February 3, 1994 and diplomatic relations were resumed in July 1995. Vietnam's new economic policy called Doi Moi (translated as 'renovation') has opened up the economy though it is still centrally controlled.

People

Vietnam's population exceeds 90 million with some 65% being under 30 years of age. The majority of the population belongs to Viet or Kinh ethnic groups but another 54 ethnic groups call Vietnam home. These include ethnic Chinese, Thai, Dao (pronounced *Zao*), Tay (or Thay), Nung, Hmong, Khmer, Cham, Jarai, Bahnar and Ede, Black Thai and Brau.

Vietnam is one of the most crowded countries in the world with population densities exceeding 200 per km² (77 sq miles) and much higher figures in the cities.

Increasing tourism arrivals to the country are boosting the economic coffers.

Vietnamese use a currency called the *dong* and many first-time travellers have difficulty in coming to grips with the hundreds of thousands of *dong* required to purchase even small and basic items (visitors can convert $US50 to become *dong* millionaires). US dollars are often quoted in large city hotels and restaurants.

The national dress for girls and women is the *ao dai*, a high neck, fitted tunic slit to the waist over loose silk pants, that resembles the Chinese *qi pao*. While young Vietnamese are increasingly adopting modern technology, many women still wear these traditional long tunics. Conical hats, called *non la* and made from dried palm leaves, are one of the iconic features of Vietnamese attire. Skilfully woven, they keep out the sun and rain. They are worn by Vietnamese everywhere and are an essential purchase for every visitor. In Hué, *non bait ho* is a version of the conical hat that is carefully woven to incorporate words of poetry.

The Dao, another large hill tribe community, are best seen around Sapa. The women are easily identified by the large red or embroidered turban often made more ornate with pom-poms. The Giay people migrated from China and the women wear clothes appropriate to their age with the older women having darker clothing than the younger. They pray to their ancestors around a small household altar.

Approximately 60% of the population is still employed in the agricultural, fishing and forestry sector of the economy and some 25% of the country is under agricultural production. Production is so successful, especially for rice, that Vietnam is the world's fifth largest producer but the second largest exporter of the valuable grain. Most rice is grown as wet rice (in *padi* fields) while some in the uplands is dry production. It is also the world's biggest exporter of coffee after Brazil.

Rubber is another agricultural activity that involves many Vietnamese who farm small plots or work for large companies who manage broad acre plantations. Latex from the rubber tree is collected after shallow incisions have been cut into the bark. This flows downwards into small cups that are collected daily by rubber tappers. With almost one million hectares (2.5 million acres), Vietnam is the world's fifth largest producer of rubber and the fourth largest exporter. Some 50% of the total production is from Binh Phuoc, Binh Duong and Tay Ninh Provinces.

Fishing is important for those who live along the coast and most major coastal towns are home to fishing fleets. Fishing is one of the most important sources of foreign exchange for Vietnam. Large nets are suspended over bodies of water, then dropped over the surface to entrap anything below. Half-spherical basket boats (*thung chai*) made from

Sapa in north-west Vietnam is one of the best places to see colourful hill tribe communities, such as the Black Hmong, Flower Hmong and Red Dao. Many women from these hill village communities ply their handicrafts around the town and while a little commercial, the villages in the surrounding hills and valleys are still home to many leading traditional lifestyles.

Vietnam's Hmong community is estimated to be 500,000 and one of the country's largest ethnic groups. Hmong communities are also located in neighbouring countries. Several groups including the White, Black, Flower, Red and Green Hmong exist and each one wears subtle variations of traditional clothing. Black Hmong live around Sapa and are identified by their black (indigo) linen inner clothing over which is worn a colourful skirt, apron and leggings. Silver jewellery and large earrings are also worn. Women from the Flower Hmong typically wear tartan or plaid head scarves.

woven bamboo are often used by fishermen operating close to shore or along rivers.

Many hill tribe communities live in permanent villages in the mountains but relocate their agricultural fields every few years through a practice called slash-and-burn agriculture. Villagers slash the forested vegetation and then burn it to release carbon to the soil to enable better crop growth. Within a few years the tropical soil is depleted and villagers have to relocate. After a few decades the land at their disposal is usually impoverished and they have to return to the secondary forest that has grown on the initial plot. Environmentalists are concerned about the destructive nature of such practices.

These people mostly lead a subsistence life using low technology and few tools. Many villagers have to walk long distances to access their market gardens in the surrounding hills or to take their produce to market.

Those living close to Sapa in north-west Vietnam farm on a more permanent basis working on terraces that have been cut into the steep slopes.

Festivals

With so many ethnic groups, there always seems to be a festival being celebrated somewhere in Vietnam. Many are religious and often national holidays are observed.

Tet Nguyen Dan (simply known as Tet) is the Vietnamese lunar New Year. It marks the beginning of spring and is celebrated in January or February when everyone returns to their home town and much of the country goes into holiday mode. Things are decorated in fiery crimson red and at midnight on the first day of the first lunar month fireworks and raucous drum beating herald in the New Year. This is

the time when the ancestral spirits return from heaven for their annual three-day visit with the family. The day coincides with the Chinese New Year and some traditions are common to both. In Vietnam, both the house and the family are cleansed in preparation for the visit by the spirits. Families gather on New Year's Eve to bid farewell to the old year and greet the new one.

While lion dances originated in China, they are also staged in Vietnam especially around Tet and Tet Trung Thu (mid-Autumn Festival).

During Tet, kumquat trees are popular decorations in many houses especially those in the north. The orange fruit symbolizes fertility and fruitfulness, both of which the family prays for in the New Year. Orange also adds a warm and bright colour to the bleakness of the northern winter. While an exciting time to be in Vietnam, visitors need to be aware that many things close and public transport during the holiday is very crowded.

Visitors to Ho Chi Minh City during Tet can see the very colourful Nguyen Hue flower road spectacle with its bright blooms and ornate decorations in the centre of the city. This attracts large crowds during the day and night as the locals clamber to pose and be photographed in front of the brightly coloured flowers.

Weddings are often selected for their auspicious dates and, at certain times of the year, the front entrance to many households is converted to a makeshift wedding reception hall where family and friends gather to wish the recently married couple the best of luck.

Opposite: Weddings are an important part of every culture. Here, the groom's family is being cycled to receive the bride at her home.

Top right: Ho Chi Minh City's flower display is a highlight of the Tet holiday.

Bottom right: Prior to the festival of Tet, kumquat shrubs are usually delivered on the back of motorbikes.

Religion

Vietnam is home to various Western and Eastern religions. An estimated 16% of Vietnamese are followers of Mahayana Buddhism. This form of Buddhism originated in India and is practised by more Buddhists around the world than the other forms of Theravada and Vajrayana Buddhism.

Opposite: Phap Bao Pagoda in Hoi An has many ornate architectural features and is surrounded by tranquil gardens.

One of the most active Buddhist temples in Ho Chi Minh City is the Thien Hau Pagoda in Cholon which was established by a congregation whose ancestors mostly originate from Canton in China.

Catholicism was introduced by French missionaries in the 16th century and has over six million followers in the country. One of the grandest churches in the country is the Notre Dame Cathedral in HCMC. Its two imposing 56-m (184-ft) high bell towers dominate the immediate skyline

Above: Thien Hau Pagoda in Cholon is a Chinese-styled temple dedicated to Thien Hau, the Lady of the Sea.

Right: Notre Dame Cathedral in Ho Chi Minh City was built from materials that were mostly imported al the way from Marseilles in France.

although skyscrapers are encroaching. Completed in 1877 it was built from imported red bricks from Marseilles and local granite rock.

Muslims make up less than 1% of the population. Islam was introduced to Vietnam by early Arab traders who journeyed to China as early as the 7th century. While the Cham are also Muslims, their religious practices are different from those of traditional Islam. There are mosques in HCMC and Hanoi; the current Saigon Central Mosque was built in the busy Dong Khoi area by Indian Muslims in 1935.

Other Vietnamese are guided through life by Confucianism which is more a philosophy than a religion. This was introduced into Vietnam when the Chinese dominated the land. One of the noted Confucian temples in the country is Hanoi's Temple of Literature, which dates back to 1070.

Dai Dao Tam Ky Pho Do (usually shortened to Cao Dai) is an interesting political-religious cult mostly confined to the provinces surrounding HCMC. It was founded in Vietnam by Ngo Van Chieu in 1926 and its name is derived from a Taoist term which means "high tower". God is referred to as a heavenly being and is depicted by a mystical eye that represents universal consciousness. The "divine eye" is a feature of all Cao Dai temples and a symbol of the religion.

Caodaiism is the outcome of an attempt to create the ideal religion by taking in the best ideas from religions and philosophies from East and West. Elements of Taoism, Buddhism, Christianity, Confucianism and other religions are incorporated in its doctrines. However, its organization is modelled on Catholicism. It has a Holy See (near Tay Ninh, north-west of HCMC) and a figurehead called Ho Phap (similar to the Pope). From its inception, Caodaiism was also a voice for Vietnam's farm workers through which they could agitate for better conditions from the French colonial masters.

The Dai Dao Tam Ki Temple just outside Da Lat on the road to the coast and Nha Trang is one of the most representative of Cao Dai architecture but there are many around HCMC especially in the Mekong Delta.

Cuisine

Vietnamese food is considered to be one of the great global cuisines. Within a few decades it has moved offshore and is now found all over the world, especially where Vietnamese migrants settled after the war.

Food is one of the best reasons for travelling to Vietnam. The country was once influenced by the Chinese and the French as well as having traded extensively with Portuguese and Indian merchants. All four cultures have left lasting impressions on Vietnamese dishes. Its cuisine has also been influenced by the hundreds of kilometres of coastline and the many rivers that dissect the land.

Above: Vietnamese cuisine is known for its subtle flavours and dipping sauces prepared to accompany specific dishes.

Opposite top: Fresh greens accompany many dishes, such as this Vietnamese pancake.

Opposite below: While rice is a staple, noodles are also commonly served.

Vietnamese food is not overly spicy but light, subtle and flavoursome. Rice is a staple and while there are other similarities to Chinese food, the use of distinctive herbs and seasoning rather than sauces in the cooking, provides its uniqueness. Vietnamese chefs have adopted noodles from China and the use of a wok for stir-fried dishes. However, fish sauce, or *nuoc mam*, is more dominant than soy sauce and many Vietnamese dishes tend to be boiled rather than stir-fried.

No Vietnamese meal is complete without herbs, either as a garnish or in their own right as an integral ingredient. Some dishes are eaten wrapped in fresh lettuce leaves with one or two herbs, such as fennel, coriander, mint, basil or dill for flavour. Many dishes are served with a side dish of cut chillies and dipping sauces for those who like extra spiciness.

Generalities aside, there are many distinctive regional variations on the theme. While Vietnamese cooking traditions were firmly entrenched before the French arrived, they left lasting legacies, so that the Vietnamese *baguettes*, coffee and *croissants* are as good as any in Paris.

Vietnam can be divided into three main culinary regions. In the north, with its harsher winters, the food is not as complex as the central region of which the former imperial capital of Hué is the main city. Many experts argue that the further south one travels, the greater the refinement in food with Ho Chi Minh City being the culinary pinnacle of the country. Others consider the food of Hué to be the best in the country as it includes many special dishes from the imperial kitchens, vegetarian dishes prepared in the temples and delicious but simple home-style cooking. A speciality

Throughout history, pepper has been very important to the spice trade and today, some 60% of the world's pepper is sourced from Vietnam. It thrives on Phu Quoc where many claim the pepper is sweeter and nuttier than elsewhere. Despite originating from India, Vietnam is now the world's largest pepper producer contributing 34% of the world trade.

Other essential ingredients used in Vietnamese cooking include star anise, dried mushrooms, chillies, ginger, coconut milk, coriander, cumin, bean curd, dried jellyfish, galangal (a type of ginger), lemongrass, turmeric, wood ear fungus and soy sauce.

Arguably Vietnam's most famous contribution to the culinary world is *pho* (pronounced *fur*), a beef or chicken and noodle broth. The noodles, called *banh pho*, are made from rice flour. They come in various widths and lengths

in central Vietnam is *banh khoai,* a crispy yellow pancake made from rice-flour and egg that is fried before shrimp, pork and bean sprouts are added. It's eaten with a sauce of peanuts and sesame seed.

One of the most famous dishes in Hanoi is *cha ca* (grilled fish with rice noodles) made from Anh Vu fish. While the fish has few bones and is very tasty, other fish are often substituted. The dish is prepared with chives, dill, turmeric, fish sauce, shrimp paste, chillies, fresh herbs and vermicelli noodles. *Cha Ca La Vong* is the most famous restaurant serving this dish in Hanoi.

Nuoc mam is a vital ingredient in Vietnamese cooking and as a condiment, often served as a dipping sauce (some 200 million litres/ 44 million gallons are produced annually). While some Vietnamese argue over the individual merits of fish sauce from Phan Thiet and Phu Quoc, all Vietnamese agree that without it, food would be very bland. It has been described as "edible perfume" despite being made in a very smelly manner using fermented fish to which salt has been added. Depending on how far north you go, the smell of the sauce is increasingly more pungent but when added to food it provides a distinctive flavour.

and are quickly cooked in boiling water or soup. This aromatic soup originates from northern Vietnam but is served all over the country and now around the world. Chicken (*pho ga*) and beef (*pho bo*) are the main styles whose broth has a distinctive star anise flavour. Ginger, cardamom, cinnamon, fish sauce and salt and pepper complement this. At the table, diners add their own fresh ingredients, such as spring onions, coriander, bean sprouts and freshly squeezed lime juice. *Pho* stalls are found all over Vietnam and are usually temporary with streetside settings of tables and low stools.

Another interesting but spicier soup is *my quang dac biet*, which is a special chicken noodle soup served with *banh ba*, or dry pancake, covered in sesame seeds. This soup is brimming with many ingredients from fat noodles to mint, dried prawns, grilled chicken, egg, peanuts and carrots. The accompanying pancakes are served along with chilli, onions, spring onions, fish sauce, thinly sliced banana flower and sprouts.

Banh trang is the Vietnamese equivalent of *ravioli* pasta. It's a round, semi-transparent, thin, hard and dry rice-paper and is used for wrapping Vietnamese translucent spring rolls (*banh cuon*) and grilled meats, with salad and herbs. It's made from a dough of finely ground rice, water and salt, with tapioca (*cassava*) flour as the binding agent. These are then put on bamboo mats to dry in the sun. Once dry, they will keep for a long time. Before consumption, they are

moistened by covering with a damp cloth until soft or by dipping quickly into warm water. To make them crisp and golden-brown colour, the wrappers are usually brushed lightly with a sugar-water solution before frying.

Spring rolls or *nem* are another well known Vietnamese food which are made by filling rolls of rice paper with mushrooms, vermicelli, vegetables and meats. These are deep fried and served with various dipping sauces including fish sauce. They are also available uncooked or fresh with prawns (*goi cuon*).

Vietnamese enjoy eating dragon fruit (which are not native to Vietnam but rather a cactus originating from Mexico, Central and South America), durians, rambutans, pomelos, nashi pears, pomegranates, mangosteens, guava, longan, jackfruit, mangoes, pineapple, papaya, bananas, watermelons, green-skinned oranges, lemons and limes. In the cooler highlands strawberries and peaches are also grown. Coconuts grow almost everywhere and make a refreshing drink in the tropical climate. Street vendors sell their fruit from baskets slung over their shoulders.

While some city folk seek out the comfort of trendy, air-conditioned restaurants, the bulk of the population eat at home, in markets or in roadside hawker stalls. Many Vietnamese buy fresh produce daily from the markets. These markets are always lively and mostly open at dawn and again at dusk as freshness is all-important to Vietnamese chefs, even those who cook at home. Often the retail action extends way beyond the confines of the market with traders setting up along the surrounding roads and footpaths. Most street food is prepared fresh from ingredients purchased that morning from the markets.

As well as the ubiquitous *pho*, popular street food includes *nem ran* (deep-fried spring rolls), *ca kho to* (stewed fish in clay pot), *chao tom* (prawn on sugar cane), *banh xeo* (crispy egg pancake with bean sprouts, shrimp and pork), *cue rang me* (stir-fried crab with tamarind sauce), *sup hat sen* (sweet lotus seed soup) and *goi buoi tom* (pomelo and chicken salad) to name a few. *Banh bao* (Chinese steamed buns usually filled with minced pork and a quail egg) are the perfect breakfast, late night snack or snack on the go.

Coffee drinking is another valued institution in the country and a legacy from the French. The beans are grown in several places including the hills around Da Lat and Buon Me Thuot. Coffee is frequently consumed in streetside stalls by patrons sitting on low stools at equally low tables. The traditional way to serve coffee is in shots obtained by passing water over ground coffee beans in an aluminium immerser placed on top of a small glass. An additional glass of tea is also served in most outlets.

Many Vietnamese also enjoy a refreshing beer after a hard day's work with several local beers being keenly sought after. These include *333* (or *bah, bah, bah*), *Bière Larue, BGI, Hanoi, Lao Cai, Halida, Saigon, Hué* and *Dai Viet*. Global brands are also available. Something uniquely Vietnamese is *bia hoi*, or new beer, which is consumed fresh and brewed daily, normally on the streets in make-shift bars which spring up all over Vietnam in the evening. Delivered to the table in plastic jugs, its low alcoholic content (3%) makes it refreshing as well as cheap.

Fruit juices and sugar cane juice are served everywhere. Long stems of purple sugar cane are passed between purpose-built crushers and the sweet juice extracted is served with ice.

Snakes have special significance for many Vietnamese as they supposedly have medicinal and aphrodisiacal properties. While wine from grapes and other fruit is made in the country, snake wine is also available as is snake soup, especially in winter. Other local wine is made from fermented or distilled rice or corn.

Opposite: 'Pho' or noodle soup comes in various forms including chicken.

Top: Fresh coconut juice is a popular and refreshing drink.

Right: Fresh fruit is important in the diets of all Vietnamese and entrepreneurial people sell it everywhere, including from boats on Halong Bay.

Habitats

Protected areas in Vietnam (natural and cultural) cover some 1.1 million ha (2.47 million acres) or 3% of the total land area. Despite the pressure on land, there are plans to extend this. Since the year 2000 eight UNESCO Biosphere Reserves have been designated in the country.

Some of the better known national parks are Cuc Phuong 222 km² (86 sq miles), Cat Tien 720 km² (280 sq miles) and Con Dao 150 km² (58 sq miles).

Forest protection is very important in Vietnam as forest coverage is under serious threat particularly in the central highlands. The apparent forest cover is now just an estimated 28% and this includes secondary forest, damaged forest and new plantations. Conversion to plantations and farmland is ongoing and illegal logging is a problem. Experts classify 40% of the land as having bare cover.

The situation was already bad enough due to the destructive effects of herbicides and defoliants used during the Vietnam War. The mountains and forests along what was known as the Ho Chi Minh Trail were natural guerrilla bases and launch sites for terrorist attacks by North Vietnamese forces against those from the south. American forces destroyed large tracts of forest to deny the opposition protective cover.

Regreening efforts have been implemented but most species are introduced and planted as monoculture plantations with the main aim being to harvest them for paper pulp manufacture.

Evergreen forests are protected in the Phu Quoc National Park to the north of the island. It is home to langurs, macaques and avian species such as the Bird of Paradise.

Lakes and Wetlands

Vietnam is a long (north to south) but narrow (east to west) country of floodplains, mountains, forests and hills. The land in the south is drained by the greatest river of Indo-China, the Mekong. Here much of the vast delta floodplain is barely above sea level. In the north, the Red River flows from the mountainous hinterland into the Gulf of Tonkin in the Eastern Sea (South China Sea). These plains often flood and while this is important in the renewal of soil nutrition, flooding usually creates short term damage and destruction.

Swamp forests formerly occupied the delta floodplains of both the Mekong and Red Rivers but these were mostly cleared for agriculture centuries ago. Coastal areas of these and many other rivers support mangroves forests which are important. Melaleuca forests are also found in the Mekong Delta.

While many wetlands were destroyed by defoliation during the war, they were replanted but now clearing for shrimp farming is creating another problem for the survival of mangroves especially in the Mekong Delta. These riverine mangroves are important spawning grounds and habitats for fish. Fish traps, especially traditional ones made from rattan, are commonly seen along riverbanks and in mangrove forests.

In the transition zone between mangroves and freshwater species, Nipa swamp forest develops. These forests thrive in low-lying muddy wetlands subjected to more freshwater inundation than saltwater. Nipa Palm (*Nypa fruticans*) is used extensively as thatching for house building and also for processing sugar and alcohol but is under threat through clearing for land reclamation and shrimp farming.

Opposite: *Areas of primary forest are under threat, with secondary forest, like this near Da Lat, being more typical.*

Right: *Nipa swamp forest lines parts of the Mekong Delta south of Ho Chi Minh City.*

There is little flat land in Vietnam and most of this has already been converted to agricultural use, especially as rice fields. The semi-evergreen, dry forests that once occupied this land have also been mostly cleared. In some parts of the country reforestation programmes have been initiated but often with introduced species, such as pine, acacia and eucalyptus.

There are few natural lakes in Vietnam but several large man-made dams which serve multiple purposes ranging from hydro-electric generation, flood mitigation, domestic water supply, tourism, recreation and irrigation. Tri An and Langa Lakes to the north-east of Ho Chi Minh City are dams which generate hydroelectricity to power much of the city.

Forests

Mountainous areas of Vietnam were once covered in evergreen forests. These occur where there is high rainfall and a relatively short dry season. A rich plant variation especially occurs in the undisturbed lower slopes. On the highest slopes (above 1,000 m/3,281 ft above sea level) the bamboo understorey grades into montane forests dominated by chestnuts and oaks with mixed conifers then to higher locations dominated by conifers.

Above: Large lakes are not common in Vietnam: Langa Lake north of Ho Chi Minh City was artificially created by the building of a dam.

Right: Thick vegetation grows where the forest canopy has been cleared due to the increased sunlight penetration.

Opposite: Limestone rocks like those of Halong Bay support plants that can survive in poor soil.

Natural conifer forests thrive on the plateau around Da Lat while many others throughout Vietnam are actually pine plantations. Pines found around Da Lat are known as the Khasi Pine (*Pinus kesiya*) which is a species that also thrives in other parts of the region. Above 1,700 m (5,577 feet) Rhododendron species appear.

Semi-evergreen or mixed deciduous forests are home to more deciduous species (those that loose their leaves) due to the greater climatic seasonality and extended dry periods. These forests are found in the central highlands and some lowlands in the southern parts of Vietnam.

Deciduous forests also occur and are low and open enabling sunlight to penetrate into the understorey where typically grasses flourish. These forests are found in the central highlands and south-central Vietnam.

Caves and Karst Topography

Karst limestone topography (distinctive landforms of weathered limestone) is particularly evident around Halong Bay. Here, tidal sea caves in the parent limestone rock are a feature of the landscape. Inland lagoons (known locally as *phongs* or *hongs)* beyond the shoreline are accessible via often inhospitable, oyster-lined, narrow cave entrancess. Because of the isolation and unfriendly terrain, much of this ecosystem was off limits to tourists until pioneering sea kayak companies, such as Vietnam Sea Kayaking Halong Bay with John Gray, pioneered the activity in 1992.

The accumulated soil on limestone is thin and nutrient-poor, so only specialized plants can survive here. However, this ecosystem has high biodiversity with many plants being adapted to specific microclimatic conditions. Palms, cycads and grasses are commonly found.

Phong Nha-Ke Bang National Park in Quang Binh Province near the border with Laos between Hué and Vinh contains over 300 caves. Recognized as a UNESCO World Heritage Site, this 85,754-ha (212,000-acre) park supports 900 plant species and 500 species of animals.

Flora and Fauna

Some 12,000 species of higher plants (not inclusive of mosses, liverworts and lichens) exist in Vietnam to make it the 16th most biologically diverse country in the world. An estimated 50% of the entire national flora is endemic and therefore only found in Vietnam.

Top: Lotus flowers of various colours are considered sacred as the beautiful blooms emerge from their muddy swamp environment.

Above: Water lilies thrive in ponds all over Vietnam.

Vietnam's animal kingdom contains an impressive 273 species of mammals, 773 birds, 80 amphibians and 180 reptiles. Some of Asia's rarest animals, such as the Javan Rhinoceros (*Rhinoceros sondaicus*), Kouprey (*Bos sauveli*), Asian Elephant (*Elephas maximus*), Indochinese Tiger (*Panthera tigris corbetti*), Eld's Deer (*Panolia eldii*), Crested Argus (*Rheinardia ocellata*) and Green Peafowl (*Pavo muticus*), are found in Vietnam. Five species of turtle are recorded in national waters and they are all classified as threatened.

The Kouprey or Grey Ox first became known to science as late as 1937 but has not been sighted since 1988 and is now thought to be extinct. This large, forest-dwelling, wild ox had its home in Cambodia and southern Laos as well as western Vietnam but hunting and forest destruction are thought to have taken their toll.

The beautiful lotus flower (*Nelumbo nucifera*) is the national flower of Vietnam and is found in wetlands and ponds all over the country. Normally pink, there are other colours, including pure white and purple. In addition to providing colour to the countryside, the root and seed pods are eaten and the flowers are used to adorn houses and for use in religious ceremonies. It has special significance for Buddhists: they use the flower as a symbol of enlightenment as it rises from the murkiest of muddy locations to mature into one of the most beautiful flowers. It therefore represents commitment, purity and optimism for the future.

Hibiscus is another commonly seen flower in Vietnam as it is frequently used for garden landscaping especially in resorts and hotels. It grows in a variety of environments

smallest of the Asian hornbills, this species is still quite large with male adults attaining a length of 70 cm (28 in). Hornbills are noted for their prominent casque (beak) which in the case of the Pied Oriental is ivory coloured. The underside of the body is white while the back is black and they also have a prominent red eye. They are omnivorous but their favourite food is the fig which they obtain from forest trees, such as those found in Cat Tien and Cat Ba National Parks.

from the more temperate parts of the country to tropical areas and birds are attracted to its showy flowers.

Vietnam is not the easiest country in the world for sighting wildlife as much of the natural vegetation has been altered. Seeing birds in cages is more common than seeing them in their natural habitat. Breeding captive birds is popular: many people are content to capture and put birds in cages to listen to their melodious tones. Forest clearing and destruction have greatly reduced Vietnam's bird population as has the habit of eating wild birds.

Rare birds, such as the Edwards's Pheasant (*Lophura edwardsi*), have recently been sighted in the forests around Hai Van Pass in central Vietnam.

The Oriental Pied Hornbill (*Anthracoceros albirostris*) is one of the region's more unusual bird species. While the

Above left: Colourful hibiscus flowers are common ornamental flowers in the gardens of Vietnam.

Above: The Oriental Pied Hornbill is native to the region including Vietnam and its distinctive beak may be as long as 16 cm (6 in).

The Cattle Egret (*Bubulcus ibis*) is commonly sighted in various habitats ranging from pastures to padi fields and grasslands as well as the shallows of wetlands. This species of heron has a wide range around the world and it can be seen near water buffalo which disturb insects while grazing. Cattle Egrets eagerly feed on these insects and often sit on the backs of the buffalo.

Raptors or birds of prey are often sighted soaring on a thermal over the islands of Halong Bay. White-bellied Sea Eagles (*Haliaeetus leucogaster*) are the most common. They are residents over a wide range that extends from Sri Lanka to Australia including Vietnam and all of Southeast Asia. Using their large yellow talons, they swoop on hapless prey and often carry it back to their large stick eyries to consume. Mating sea eagles are monogamous and stay with the same partner until one dies. Interestingly, the female is slightly larger than the male.

Visitors to Vietnam are most likely to see more domesticated animals than those in the wild. Domesticated Asian Water Buffalo (*Bubalus bubalis*) are commonly seen throughout rural Vietnam wallowing in muddy ponds, grazing on the verges of roads or rice fields, being used to pull ploughs or sometimes as beasts of burden to pull carts.

In the wild, the most commonly seen primate is the Long-tailed Macaque (*Macaca fascicularis*) which occurs in forests and wetlands throughout the region. Also known as the Crab-eating Macaque, it is an omnivore which does eat crabs, but rarely. These social animals live in groups with several females, their offspring and at least one dominant male. They occur throughout the country: Cat Tien National Park in the south and Bai Tu Long National Park in the northeast are two good locations for sightings.

One of several endangered species in Vietnam is the Vietnamese Sika Deer (*Cervus nippon pseudaxis*) which is a subspecies of the more widely distributed Sika Deer (*Cervus nippon*). It is smaller than other subspecies and was previously recorded in northern Vietnam but it is now considered extinct in the wild although reintroduction programmes are being conducted.

Above: Long-tailed Macaques have a matrilineal social group with a female dominance hierarchy.

Left: The Sika Deer is found in Vietnam and its name is derived from 'shika', the Japanese word for deer.

Opposite top left: As with many raptors, the female White-bellied Sea Eagle is slightly larger than the male.

Opposite top right and below: Cattle Egrets and Water Buffalo have a symbiotic relationship whereby the grazing buffalo disturbs insects that the bird consumes and in return, the bird rids the cattle of ticks.

Arts and Crafts

Vietnamese artists are highly skilled and art galleries are common in the big cities especially as the pieces of art are most affordable. Communist revolutionary art and posters are particularly popular with collectors and older pieces often fetch a high price.

Baskets are important in the daily lives of the Vietnamese: rattan and bamboo are used to make carrying baskets, storage baskets and those for containing food. Basketmakers weave long strips of pliable green forest products into a range of utilitarian items and in hill tribe communities, the smoke from the hearth seasons these materials. Baskets with wooden frames are especially important in rural areas for carrying produce from the fields to market. Rattan and bamboo are now also used for producing an extensive range of woven household products.

Above: Intricately woven baskets are both functional and decorative.

Above right: Vietnamese lacquerware is sold in the main tourist districts and makes an ideal souvenir.

Lacquerware originates from China but the Vietnamese have become expert exponents of the art, producing ornate and utilitarian items made from lacquer which is a resin extracted from the Rhus tree. Fine lacquerware is produced over an extended period by adding multiple layers of paint to a frame. This is sanded after each coat has dried making the final coat very smooth and shiny. Much of what is sold on the streets of Vietnam is mass produced and made for the tourists – antique pieces being very expensive.

Hand-embroidered pictures offer a snapshot of Vietnamese life. These photo-perfect pieces of delicately hand-worked fabrics are stitched from cotton or silk. Silks and cottons are also woven into fabric on traditional looms. Ha Dong, on the outskirts of Hanoi is the home of sericulture and silk fabrics. The material is made into items such as clothing, household accessories and lantern shades which are sold throughout the country.

Vietnam's various colourful hill tribe communities have their own unique and ornate traditional clothing. In some of these communities, the women especially continue to wear such clothing although many younger members have adopted more western-style dress.

Hand-embroidered and woven textiles are still produced in many communities and make popular souvenir items. These can be purchased in tourist destinations, such as Sapa and Da Lat, where it is also possible to see the textiles being produced. While commercial dyes are commonly used these days, some tribes still use traditional dyes sourced

from barks, leaves and roots. Indigo is still used by Hmong and Dao tribes as witnessed by the tell-tale signs of blueish fingers on the hands of the women selling textiles around Sapa. Indigo is traditionally used to dye everyday and farmer's clothing.

Some textiles are still hand-stitched while others are woven on looms using weighted heddles or on back-strap looms. Patterns have often been handed down from generation to generation and a good weaver will set up the pattern on her loom from memory alone.

Left: There are many talented artists in Vietnam who produce colourful pieces of art.

Above: The women in many hill tribe communities are skilful weavers.

Sports and Lifestyles

Trekking around Sapa is one of the best ways to start exploring the mountainous north-west and the various ethnic hill communities that live there. Sapa is the perfect base to kit up and seek the services of a range of professional trekking companies located in the main street of this small mountainous town. Industrious local hill tribe women also offer their services in enabling tourists to visit their villages and homes.

Local and international trekking companies also offer biking tours of the country. Visitors get to experience firsthand the sights, sounds and aromas of the country for periods extending from a few hours to over a week. These companies provide an experienced guide, mountain bikes and a back-up truck and bus as well as organize the logistics in providing access to Vietnam's highways and byways.

While SCUBA diving in Vietnam is not the region's best, there are still a few sites to explore especially around Nha Trang and the island of Phu Quoc. The best time for diving off the south-central coast is from March to September.

Birdwatching is best done in national parks, such as Cat Tien in the south, Bach Ma in the centre and Cuc Phuong in the north.

Watersports, such as kayaking, are popular in most seaside resorts like Nha Trang and around the picturesque Halong Bay. Operators conduct one- to six-day excursions around the bay and adventurous travellers using the specially designed sea kayaks gain access to the unique limestone features. As camping is not permitted in Halong Bay, kayakers spend each night on a traditional local junk.

Golf is still a relatively new sport in Vietnam and only accessible to affluent members of society. Golf tourism is developing with some 25 courses in the country and a staggering 65 on the drawing board. Leading international golf course designers, such as Sir Nick Faldo, Greg Norman and Colin Montgomerie, have been recruited to weave their golfing magic through various Vietnamese landscapes.

Opposite top: Trekking in places like Sapa is best done with a local guide.

Opposite below: Kayaking around the islands of Halong Bay offers a unique view of the limestone topography.

Above: An aerial view of the 9th hole at the Laguna Lăng Cô Resort. Several coastal resorts have incorporated golf courses into their range of facilities.

Chapter 2: The North

Northern Vietnam extends north and north-west from the capital Hanoi to the borders with China and Laos. The Red River drains waters which flow down from the mountains especially those in the far north-west. The scenery from the beautiful, forest-covered, limestone islands, bays and coves of Halong Bay to the rice terraces around Sapa is what attracts most tourists.

Hanoi

Vietnam's capital and second largest city, Hanoi (also spelt Ha Noi), is situated on the southern banks of the Red River 88 km (55 miles) inland from the coast and the Gulf of Tonkin in the Eastern Sea (South China Sea). Hanoi has been settled for over 1,000 years and its heritage is one of its most valuable tourism assets. With over six million residents, the narrow inner city streets are congested but so far, it has retained much of its historic charm.

Above right: Hanoi's streets are constantly busy with traders, such as bamboo basket sellers, plying their wares from the back of bicycles.

Right: Hanoi is a beautiful city with lakes and several charming old parts. The French and Old Quarters are the most fascinating to explore on foot or in the comfort of a cyclo. The 36 trade streets forming a maze in the Old Quarter take their name from the fact that they were once home to a specific trade (such as silk weaving, pottery, goldsmithing and gravestone carving). This green oasis lies between the Red River and Hoan Kiem Lake.

Left: The French Quarter was built from 1887 to 1954 when the city was the capital of French Indo-China. Tree-lined boulevards are home to grand colonial public buildings, such as the Opera House (pictured), villas and Vietnamese temples. Two hotels in the vicinity have adopted sympathetic architecture to blend into the colonial surroundings. Check into the Hilton Hanoi Opera or MGallery Hotel de l'Opera Hanoi to enjoy colonial exteriors and contemporary interiors.

Below and right: Hoan Kiem Lake is in the middle of the city while the larger West Lake (Tay Ho) lies outside the centre. Hoan Kiem lakeside is always busy with people exercising at dawn and dusk, children playing and others crossing the ornate red wooden bridge to visit the 17th century Ngoc Son Temple on the north-eastern side.

Left: Within walking distance of Ngoc Son Temple is the Thang Long Water Puppet Theatre. The art of water puppetry originated in the Red River Delta and dates back to the 11th century. Performances feature lacquerware puppets and are staged in waist-deep water.

Right: Coffee is very important in the lives of Hanoi's citizens and many home-grown concepts have opened. One of Hanoi's most charming is the 'Hapro Coffee Kiosk' at the southern end of Hoan Kiem Lake under the shade of mature trees near the water's edge. It's the perfect place for watching people, enjoying a 'ca phe sua da' (iced white coffee) and reading the 'Viet Nam News'.

Left: Ho Chi Minh Mausoleum is always packed with mostly Vietnamese visitors queueing up to pay their respects to their much-loved former leader whose embalmed body is on display.

Below left: The rebuilt Dong Xuan Market (it was destroyed in a 1994 fire) is always a hive of activity and just south of the market on Cau Dong Street crabs served with citrus are a speciality.

Below right: Ho Chi Minh's modest stilt home can be found behind the grandiose palace and was the then-president's preferred place of residence. It's now a museum and a popular venue to visit as it has been maintained as if 'Uncle Ho' was still there.

Above: Hanoi's Temple of Literature is the site of Vietnam's first university. Dating back to 1070, it features some rare examples of traditional Vietnamese architecture. Its gardens and pavilions make it a pleasant retreat but as it is a popular stop on most city tours, it is usually packed with inquisitive tourists and locals. There are five courtyards and its entrance gate has an ancient sign in Vietnamese requesting that visitors dismount from their horses before entering.

Right: Hanoi Zoo and surrounding Thu Le Park offer a tranquil garden setting that makes a pleasant respite from the busy street life of the capital. The zoo takes a multi-functional approach to catering to visitors, so that rides, shops, restaurants and traders selling a variety of fun-fair goodies are as much a part of the zoo as are the animals. There are, in fact, not that many animals housed here and most are behind restrictive bars that limit visibility.

Around Hanoi

Right: One of the most popular trips from the capital is to the riverine setting of the Perfume Pagoda, 60 km (37 miles) to the south of Hanoi near the town of My Duc. This is a trip in which the journey is as fascinating as the destination as visitors travel by boats rowed by women, up the picturesque floodplain lined by limestone cliffs to reach the base of Huong Tich Mountain that houses the main Buddhist pagoda. For many tourists the riverboat ride and a few pagodas near the boat terminal is the full extent of their visit. Buddhist devotees take the steep 4-km (2½-mile) uphill climb to pray at the pagoda. It is best to avoid the Perfume Pagoda during Buddhist festivals as the river and mountain climb are very crowded.

Above: Handicrafts are important in Vietnam and the various villages around Hanoi have become tourist attractions as well as a source of traditional artisan-made handicrafts. These include Dong Ky (inlaid furniture), Bat Trang (ceramics) and Van Vuc (silk).

Above: The port and industrial city of Haiphong is the third largest urban area in Vietnam. While it was extensively bombed during the war, many French colonial buildings survived, such as the one now housing the Haiphong Museum (pictured). Trains connect the city with Hanoi and some tourists depart from here for a boat trip to Halong Bay.

The North-east and Halong Bay

The far north-east of Vietnam is often referred to as the cradle of Vietnamese civilization since much of the nation's history was written here. It has also been the part of Vietnam most influenced by China which is to the immediate north. The Red River drains through the area and brings life to the farmers who live along and near its banks. Vietnam's largest seaport of Haiphong lies at the mouth of the Red River.

Looking like a Vietnamese painting, Halong (also spelt Ha Long) Bay, 160 km (110 miles) east of Hanoi, is dotted with jagged limestone islands that rise from the emerald green waters. Halong Bay's limestone topography indicates that the area was once inundated by a vast sea. This sedimentary rock is rich in the mineral calcite and has evolved over millions of years from the accumulation of the skeletal fragments of marine organisms, such as corals. Typically it is grey, hard and crystalline often with sharp, jagged edges and ridges. These rocks form the backbone of the islands dotting the bay and steep cliffs rising from the waterline are the characteristic landform. As the large limestone blocks weather, the tops of these islands become rounded and within the rocks, water erodes along cracks and fault lines to create caves, caverns and grottoes.

Left: *Vietnam's natural beauty is typified by the limestone karst topography of Halong Bay. Although much of the Oscar-award-winning, 1992 French movie 'Indochine' was shot in Malaysia, Halong Bay's picturesque scenery featured prominently. Halong Bay National Protected Area, a UNESCO World Heritage Site, covers an area of 1,553 km² (600 sq miles) and includes 1,969 islands. The landscape is ever-evolving as the erosional forces of nature continue to sculpt the limestone rock and the caves and the rivers that run through it.*

A cruise around the bays and coves is one of Vietnam's most popular tours. Some 300 boats based at Bai Chay Tourist Wharf do a brisk trade in ensuring a steady flow of tourists gains access to the waters. While many cruise the 100-km (62-mile) long waterway during daylight hours, others make an overnight trip or a stay of several nights touring the bay.

This page: Cat Ba is the largest island in Halong Bay and its pleasant beaches and national park appeal to visitors. The bay is also home to some 1,000 fishing folk and their families grouped in various communities. They live on boats and floating wooden houses and survive on fishing, tourism and operating floating aquaculture farms. Children in these communities even attend floating schools.

Left and below left: Over time, the powerful erosional force of percolating water within the rocks along cracks and fault lines creates caves, caverns and grottoes that contain stalactites and stalagmites, and are home to bats and swallows. 'Hongs' are formed where the ceiling of a cave has collapsed to reveal a protected and open stretch of water, accessible via a sea cave and lined with steep cliffs.

Above: The Golden-headed Leaf Monkey (Cat Ba Langur) lives amongst the limestone forests of Cat Ba Island (a UNESCO Biosphere Reserve) and remains one of the world's most endangered primates. One of the rare plants found here is the Halong Fan Palm and many varieties of coral thrive in the bay.

The North-west

Vietnam's north-west bordering China and Laos is one of the most mountainous parts of the country. The Hoang Lien Son mountain range moderates the lowland temperature to provide refreshingly cool summers and cold winters. Ascending Vietnam's highest peak Mount Fansipan (3,142 m/ 10,308 ft) is a rigorous activity and, like all other walks here, is best done with an experienced guide as the climb is long and can be treacherous in parts.

Right and below: The area is home to colourful hill tribe people (known to the French as 'montagnards') including the Red Dao and Black Hmong. Most of the ethnic people, especially the women and children, still wear intricately woven and colourful clothing making the Sunday market in nearby Bac Ha exciting, if a little commercial these days.

Opposite: Walking in the hills from village to village is a popular activity. Walkers pass through picturesque rice terraces, fields of corn and grazing water buffalo.

Sapa

Sapa is the north-west's best known mountain retreat. Most visitors arrive on the overnight train from Hanoi via Lao Cai near the border with Yunnan Province in China. While the train is very comfortable, some guests like to travel in style in the luxuriously appointed and privately owned Victoria Express carriages. Sapa is 325 km (202 miles) from Hanoi and 1,524 m (5,000 ft) above sea level, so that it is pleasantly cool in summer. Located to the south-west of Sapa, Dien Bien Phu was the scene of a fierce and famous battle between French and local Viet Minh forces in 1954.

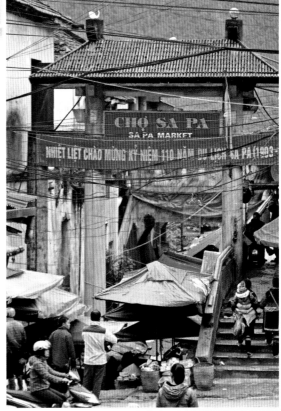

Above and opposite below: *Sapa really is a cool resort in terms of both ambiance and temperature. Like Da Lat, it was identified by the French colonialists who established it in 1922 as a health resort or hill station to escape from the lowland heat.*

Right: *Women from the hill tribes sell their wares all over town while the Sapa Market is a good place to look for souvenirs. There is a market every day but Saturday is the busiest due to the influx of tourists at the weekend. There are the usual fresh produce sections as well as hill tribe products, trekking equipment and utilitarian items for sale. Some of the embroidery is machine-made while the authentic textiles are still hand-stitched and more expensive.*

Opposite top: *Sapa is also home to several colourful hill tribe communities. Dao women (pronounced 'yao') wear simple red head scarves or ornate ones like this with silver coins and tassels. Traditionally, the red dye was obtained from the root of a local tree.*

Chapter 3: Central Vietnam

Central Vietnam is a long, narrow, coastal stretch of over 1,000 km/620 miles from Vinh in the north to Phan Rang in the south. It includes the main towns of Hué, Danang, Hoi An, Da Nang Beach and Nha Trang. While most offer cultural attractions, beaches are never too far away.

Hué

Hué has a degree of refinement having once been the nation's imperial city. While much of the city was destroyed in fierce battles during the Vietnam War, it has resurrected itself and is now a pleasant city of lakes, canals and wide, tree-lined boulevards.

This page: South of the city along Perfume River, the Tombs of the Emperors of the Nguyen Dynasty and Thien Mu Pagoda (left) are Hué's other main attractions. Many of the older tombs are crumbled ruins but those of Khai Dinh Hue (above), Minh Mang and Tu Duc are still grand structures.

Right: Shallows along the coast north of Danang are home to fishing communities who use traditional bamboo structures to trap fish.

Centre: The Complex of Hué Monuments, of which the Imperial City is the principal site, is recognized as a UNESCO World Heritage Site. The Imperial City or Citadel, built in 1804 once served as the primary residence of the royal family and housed offices for the heads of state. This expansive walled and moated property is a fortress and palace covering a huge area that includes the Purple Forbidden City.

Left: At 1,172 m (3,845 ft) and 20 km (12 miles) long, Hai Van Pass, snaking between Hué and Danang, is Vietnam's highest and longest pass. It separates the country geographically and climatically as the cold winds from the north rarely penetrate further south than the pass. While the most scenic road weaves over the pass, the train line skirts the coast – these are two of Vietnam's most acclaimed and picturesque journeys. Just further west is the cooling, French-era hill station within what is now Bach Ma National Park.

Lang Co

Long sandy beaches are common along a coastal stretch of 130 km (80 miles) from Hoi An to Hué. A road tunnel beneath the Hai Van Pass ensures that the journey to Lang Co (60 km/37 miles) for guests arriving into central Vietnam via Danang International Airport takes under an hour.

Right: Several hotels line the beachfront and now Vietnam's first integrated resort could be the development to place Lang Co on the world travel stage. Laguna Lăng Cô is a 280-ha (692-acre) site currently with two luxury resorts, the Banyan Tree Lăng Cô and Angsana Lăng Cô but with space for another six. In the centre of the development just to the north of Lang Co is the Sir Nick Faldo-designed, championship 18-hole golf course. It is flanked on one side by the ocean and Canh Duong Beach and on the other by the foothills of the surrounding mountains. Golfers appreciate that with features, such as streams, padi fields and the tropical surroundings, they are playing in uniquely Vietnamese surroundings. Spas, restaurants and an extensive range of recreational activities on the land and water ensure the property provides a complete holiday.

Left: Lang Co situated between Hué and Danang is one of the finest beaches. Here, the narrow strip of sand and isthmus are backed by a large lagoon and the once sleepy but picturesque village has been earmarked for tourism development.

Demilitarized Zone (DMZ)

Between 1954 and 1975 the Ben Hai River (on the 17th parallel) in Quang Tri Province of central Vietnam served as the border between North and South Vietnam. While this Demilitarized Zone or DMZ was supposedly a military-free zone, there was a strong military presence and fierce fighting here during the American War in Vietnam. Some of the bloodiest battle sites of the war are located just to the south of the DMZ and Hollywood movies, such as *Hamburger Hill*, were based on these locations and battles. Former battlefields and parts of the Ho Chi Minh Trail attract adventurous travellers who use Hué, Dong Ha or Dong Hoi as a base.

Above: Quang Tri Provincial Museum in Dong Ha has a good collection of United States aircraft and tanks such as a Cessna A-37 Dragonfly and Bell UH-1 Iroquois ('Huey') helicopter from the war. Cultural and historic features of the province are also housed inside the museum building. There is a more open museum located at the former military airport of Ta Com near Khe Sanh.

Above: A road extends from Dong Ha to Lao Bao on the border with neighbouring Laos. Hill people from the Van Kieu race live and farm in the forested hills. These people are related to other communities in Cambodia, Laos and Thailand, with those living in Dakrong village near Khe Sanh being Christians. They practise shifting cultivation, which means they relocate their fields to recently cleared forest every few years. Some villages also maintain permanent rice fields where wet rice is cultivated.

Danang

Danang, the fourth largest city of over one million residents, has been a strategic port city since the first millennium. It lies on the banks of the Han River and has beautiful beaches, tree-lined boulevards and great restaurants. It is refreshingly cooled by breezes from the Eastern Sea (South China Sea).

Below: The 731-m (2400-ft) long Tran Thi Ly Bridge across the Han River opened in March 2013 and is a striking new landmark for Danang, characterized by its chic red cables.

Opposite top left and right: Several archaeological sites surround Danang leading the French to establish the Museum of Cham Sculpture here, one of the city's main attractions. It houses the world's foremost collection of Cham sculptures – some 300 pieces of terracotta and carved sandstone. Champa art incorporates elements of Hinduism and Buddhism imagery. The structure itself is a grand French colonial building dating back to 1915. Other buildings in the city to visit include Danang Cathedral, Caodai Temple, Ho Chi Minh Museum and various pagodas.

Above and right: Visitors fly into Danang International Airport 2.5 km (1½ miles) south-west of the city centre. The new airport has opened up this part of Central Vietnam to international tourists and this in turn has lead to the building of hotels, such as the Grand Mercure Danang (right) and the Pullman Danang Beach Resort (above), that offer the finest international standards.

Hoi An and Da Nang Beach

Vietnam's ancient port of Hoi An 30 km (20 miles) south of Danang is one of the best preserved ports of its kind in Asia. Once a stopping point for boats from China, Japan, Portugal, Holland, France and the Middle East, it is now a magnet for tourists who come to marvel at this well-preserved riverside town with its historic, car-free core. In its heyday from the 17th to the 19th centuries, Hoi An rivalled Melaka (Malaysia) and Macau (China) as the region's most dominant port.

This page: Some 800 historic buildings miraculously survived the Vietnam War and are now protected as the Hoi An Ancient Town UNESCO World Heritage Site situated beside the Thu Bon River. To date, the city remains mostly unchanged and free of development. This living museum enables visitors to see how life was centuries ago as well as some of the trades that were conducted then and are still important.

Left: *Of the historic buildings, the most significant is the Japanese Covered Bridge. Built in the 1590s, the bridge and associated temple are the perfect combination of function and form.*

Centre: *Beaches lining the coast are just five kilometres (three miles) downriver from Hoi An at Cua Dai. This is the southernmost extent of the Da Nang Beach strip and where resorts, such as the Victoria and Swiss-Belhotel, are to be found. Da Nang Beach is divided into several sections each with its own local name. The most popular is My Khe just north of the imposing Marble Mountains with its five outcrops. Luxury resorts, such as the Furama, Hyatt Regency and Nam Hai, line this strip and there is golf at the Montgomerie Links.*

Below: *Fishermen still work off Da Nang Beach often using traditional circular rattan baskets covered in tar or varnish as boats, called 'thúng chai'.*

Nha Trang

Vietnam's best developed resort city is Nha Trang on the South Central coast. It has long been popular with local holidaymakers and now an increasing number of international tourists have discovered the long sweeping bay of golden sand here. Nha Trang Beach is not dissimilar to many other Asian resort destinations with its umbrellas, cafés, bars, massages and the inevitable trinket sellers. While it is a year-round holiday destination, the rain in November and December can put a dampener on things.

Nha Trang's beachfront, luxurious resorts and associated dining, shopping and nightlife appeal to many travellers. The city has been transformed from a sleepy fishing backwater less than two decades ago to a one-stop seaside holiday destination.

The beach is a marine playground with para sailing, jet skiing, diving, snorkelling and swimming all available. Vinpearl Water Park and Amusement Park offer a range of activities including slides and pools, and especially appeals to children and families.

Offshore, the Hon Mun Marine Protected Area is an important ecological site and area of biodiversity. Established in 2001, it aims to support both the coral reefs and the associated marine life that are important for the whole ecosystem and the fisheries industry. Swimming, snorkelling and scuba diving are available in the protected area and around the Cau, Vung, Noc, Rom and Mun islands as well as the main island called Hon Tree (or Tre) that is located just off the main Nha Trang Beach.

Left and opposite: Nha Trang has blossomed as a beachside destination with resorts like the Evason Ana Mandara (pictured) built immediately on the beach.

Below: Less than a few decades ago, the principal economic activity in Nha Trang was fishing. Fishing is still important to the community as is indicated by the large fleet moored in the sheltered mouth of Cai River just below Po Nagar Towers. Views of the fleet are best had from either the towers or the Tran Phu Bridge.

Below: To dine on seafood is another good reason for visiting Nha Trang. The best place to check out the variety available is at the lively Dam Market in the far north of the city near the Cai River, with some of the retailing spilling over into the surrounding streets.

Above and top: Tall beachside resorts, such the Sheraton Nha Trang Hotel and Spa, now represent the new face of the city's tourism. Being the holiday location that it is, there are many places in the evening to take in the seaside ambiance. 'Altitude' on the hotel's 28th floor is home to one of the city's coolest bars, if not the highest. Refreshed by sea breezes and with beautiful views across the bay, it's a popular evening spot.

Above: While Nha Trang has only been discovered by holidaymakers for a little over a decade, it has a history dating back many centuries when it was part of the Champa Kingdom that ruled Vietnam from the 7th to the early 19th century. There are several relicts of the Cham people in and around Nha Trang, the best of which are the Po Nagar Towers just north of the Cai River and overlooking the bay. Central Vietnam's coastal plain is one of the few parts of Vietnam where Hinduism made inroads.

Right: 100 km (62 miles) to the south near Phan Rang is another fine Cham building, the Po Klong Garai Cham Towers located high on a rocky hill and surrounded by cactus plants in the medieval Cham principality of Panduranga.

Central Highlands

Mountains form a backdrop to Central Vietnam's long coastline. Located at between 1,500 and 2,000 m (4,921 and 6,562 ft) above sea level and 300 km (186 miles) north of Ho Chi Minh City, Da Lat (or Dalat) is the highlands' principal tourist destination. This quaint retreat was initially used as a sanitarium by Swiss-born doctor, Alexandre Yersin. The French established the hill station here for expatriates to escape the heat and humidity of the lowlands and development began in earnest after the First World War. Da Lat is a little piece of Europe in the Vietnamese central highlands. Visitors can fly into Da Lat Airport 30 km (18½ miles) south of the town or drive the four-hour journey from Ho Chi Minh City. The town is lined with old buildings and makes an excellent base for heading out into the surrounding hills for a little trekking and to see hill tribe communities.

Above right: Da Lat was originally accessible by the old Crémaillère Railway (a cog-wheel railway) that connected Da Lat to Thap Cham 84 km (52 miles) away on the coast. While the track is closed, it's worth visiting the Art Deco train station and taking a short round-trip on a small branch line to the village of Trai Mat eight kilometres (five miles) away.

Right: Much of the mountains and escarpment around Da Lat is covered in forests that include ferns and pine trees.

Right and below: The heritage hotel of choice here is the Da Lat Palace Luxury Hotel and Golf Club that overlooks the man-made Xuan Huong Lake. The hotel dates back to 1922 and the picturesque course was once the exclusive domain of the last emperor Bao Dai but is now accessible to all. It is considered one of Vietnam's 'must-play' courses set amongst the city's hills and lakes. It includes 18 landscaped holes and an authentic 1930s clubhouse.

Above right: Many visitors come merely to stroll around the streets, linger in the cafés and enjoy the highland coffee. Coffee is traditionally served with an aluminium filter perched on top of a glass. One of the most atmospheric coffee houses in town is 'Café Tung', which is locked in a 1950s' time warp.

Left: While dragonfruit is one of the best known fruits associated with Vietnam, the cooler weather in the mountains provides perfect growing conditions for strawberries. The best place to buy them and various strawberry products is in the market where flowers are also sold. Dalat Wine made from grapes grown along the coast is sold all over the country.

Above: Market gardens are well suited to the high altitude and cool environment of the mountains around Da Lat situated 120 km (75 miles) from the coast. Cool-climate vegetables, such as peas, radishes, carrots, peppers, cabbages, lettuce, spinach, corn and bamboo shoots, thrive in the rich mountainous soil.

Right: Fruit, such as strawberries, persimmons, peaches, plums and blackcurrants, are also grown and sold around the district. Avocadoes are another treat to seek out. Many local holidaymakers travel to Da Lat to buy and enjoy these delicacies as they are cheaper than in the lowland markets. The best place to see the range of produce is in Da Lat Central Market in the middle of the town or on the stalls in front of the Thien Vuong Pagoda.

Above: Hill tribe communities or 'montagnards' live in the central highlands including an area just north of Da Lat. There are 33 distinct communities in the region with a population of 5,000 around Da Lat alone. In the local Lat language, 'Da Lat' means 'river of the Lat people'. The hamlet of Lat at the base of Lang Bian Mountain is not only home to Lat people but also to those from the Koho, Ma and Chill tribes who all communicate in their own dialect. These farming communities grow rice, beans, sweet potatoes and coffee. Traditional Lat homes are built on stilts with a wooden floor and thatched roof but these are rare nowadays as most people in the village choose to live in more modern homes. There are still examples of older style houses in the village that front onto dirt roads with many having small agricultural plots close by.

Above right: Prenn Falls to the south of the town is one of the district's most accessible waterfalls. Its landscaped gardens and 15-m (50-ft) falls and pond provide a tranquil retreat. A cable car journey over the falls offers a unique view of the forest and falls (see page 8).

Right: Some local people maintain their cotton-weaving traditions and make various items to sell to the steady stream of tourists who mostly visit in the afternoons when the villagers have returned from tending their crops some distance away.

Phan Thiet and Mui Ne

The Phan Thiet–Mui Ne strip of sandy beaches lies at the far south of Central Vietnam and just three hours (200 km, 124 miles) from Ho Chi Minh City by road. The small provincial town of Phan Thiet and its beaches are more peaceful and relaxed than Vietnam's other beachside resorts. It's just beginning to be noticed by international visitors and is destined for more development.

Opposite top: Phan Thiet is famous in Vietnam for its fish sauce (nuoc mam), available in various flavours. Chefs may argue over the relative merits of this and the fish sauce from Phu Quoc but lovers of Vietnamese food cherish both, since fish sauce is an essential ingredient of many dishes. The sauce is produced all over this seaside town situated along the Ca Ty and Muong Man Rivers. It's made from fermented fish mixed with sea salt and has a distinctive smell that wafts throughout the town. A fishing fleet of some 2,500 vessels brings in the valuable catch for processing.

Left: Van Thuy Tu Temple was built in 1762 in honour of a legendary whale that, it was believed, protected fishermen during bad weather. A 22-m (72-ft) long whale skeleton is housed here.

Below: While Mui Ne is the region's better known beach resort, there is a long picturesque beach at Phan Thiet that is popular with the locals at sunrise.

Right: One of the main reasons visitors come here is to play golf, as it is home to arguably one of Vietnam's finest golf courses: Ocean Dunes Golf Club. Opened in June 1996, the par 72 championship links-styled course of 6,149 m (6,725 yards) was designed by Sir Nick Faldo. The coconut palm and casuarina-lined course has a long list of golfing credentials with the par 3, ninth hole being noted as one of 'The World's Best 500 Holes' (Golf Magazine U.S.A.). It is also consistently voted as Vietnam's best par 3 hole. The adjoining DuParc Phan Thiet Ocean Dunes and Golf Resort is a delightful beachside resort with superb facilities.

Left: Just to the north, Mui Ne Beach is home to several international-standard resorts. The red undulating sand dunes at Hon Rom just north of Mui Ne are popular for sand boarding.

Chapter 4: The South

Southern Vietnam extends from the pulsating economic centre of Ho Chi Minh City southward to the Mekong Delta. The city is one of the main air gateways and because of the country's geography many visitors arrive here, then head north and fly home from Hanoi.

Ho Chi Minh City

Ho Chi Minh City (Saigon), Vietnam's largest city, is a re-energized and revitalized city of over nine million residents. Once the capital of South Vietnam, April 30, 1975 when North Vietnamese tanks crushed the gates of the Independence Palace to end the war and reunify the nation now seems a long while ago. Today the city is vastly different from the one badly damaged during the war. Skyscrapers rise above the city and in the streets below hundreds of thousands of motorcyclists reflect the growth and economic optimism of the young generation.

This page: The skyline of Ho Chi Minh City, particularly that of the downtown District 1, is rapidly changing as tall buildings reach ever skyward. Despite this, many streets are still lined with trees that provide shade from the tropical heat.

Left and below: The Reunification Palace (Hoi Truong Thong Nhat), once the symbol of the South Vietnam Government, has been retained almost as it was in the 1960s. The roof was used as a helipad in April 1975, enabling a massive evacuation of staff just before the palace was overrun by soldiers from the north.

Left: There are several tourist attractions including the Museum of Vietnamese History (pictured) housed in an old French colonial building near the zoo. However, it is the War Remnants Museum (formerly the Museum of American War Crimes) that is most popular with foreign visitors. It provides a chilling reminder of the American War in Vietnam. Armoured vehicles, weapons and other war paraphernalia are displayed.

Right and opposite top: The city is situated on the Saigon River 80 km (50 miles) inland. Many attractions are near the river in District 1 and include several beautiful colonial buildings, such as the Ho Chi Minh City Town Hall, General Post Office (opposite top), Opera House and Notre-Dame Cathedral (right).

Opposite below left: The city's historic hotels of the Caravelle, Continental, Rex and Majestic have been saved, rejuvenated and restored. It was the Continental Hotel that featured in the Hollywood movie 'The Quiet American' based on the Graham Greene novel of the same name. Rooftop bars are popular in the city but none has more nostalgia than that at the Rex Hotel (pictured) as wartime journalists would gather here daily to be briefed on the war by the military and possibly have a refreshing beer or two. Gleaming new hotels, such as the Sofitel, the Novotel Saigon Centre and the Pullman Saigon, are symbols of economic growth and healthy tourism arrivals.

Above: Markets selling fresh produce and food are an important part of the city's landscape: Ben Thanh Market is the biggest and most popular with locals and tourists. Built by the French as a municipal marketplace, it now offers an extensive selection of local souvenirs, fresh produce, imported goods and tasty treats. Freshly ground local coffee is a popular item, especially the hard-to-get and expensive 'ca phe chon' (weasel coffee).

Right: A landmark building, the People's Committee Hall (formerly the City Hall or Hotel de Ville de Saigon) was built between 1902 and 1908. Since 1975 it has served as the Headquarters for the HCMC People's Committee and is not open to the public.

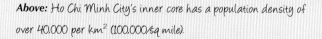

Above: Ho Chi Minh City's inner core has a population density of over 40,000 per km² (100,000/sq mile).

Right: One of the most impressive buildings is the Municipal Theatre of Ho Chi Minh City or the Saigon Opera House. This fine example of French colonial architecture was built in 1897. Initially an 800-seat theatre, it became the Assembly of the Lower House of South Vietnam until 1956 but reverted to the Opera House in 1975. It stands in front of the famous Caravelle Hotel which was once home to foreign correspondents during the war.

Above and left: Cholon or District 5, just 5 km (3 miles) west of District 1, is often referred to as the city's Chinatown as it retains many Chinese features from its temples and architecture to its food stalls. It dates back to the 18th century when people from China's southern provinces settled here. The name translates as 'big market' and the district offers a dazzling array of dining options. It is also home to the gigantic Cho Ray Hospital. Discover the best of Cholon by visiting the large central market (pictured) which is lively, busy, hot and crowded but always fascinating. It is mostly popular for local shoppers who come to purchase their fresh daily requirements, especially ingredients for cooking.

Left: While HCMC still retains many elements of its past and of traditional life, most young Vietnamese want to emulate their counterparts in the West. District 1, on the western side of the Saigon River is the area considered by the locals as downtown or the CBD (Central Business District). Here, Dong Khoi Street (pictured) is considered the most fashionable, lined as it is with cafés and international designer brands that especially appeal to the young and trendy. Neighbouring streets, such as Hai Ba Trung, Thi Sach, Le Thanh Ton and Thai Van Lung, are also experiencing rapid transformation.

Mekong Delta and South

One of Asia's great rivers, the Mekong, ends its 4,350-km (2,703-mile) long journey from its source in China's Tibetan Plateau when it flows into the Eastern Sea (South China Sea) off Vietnam. Being the world's 12th longest river, it is a valuable resource for millions of people in China, Myanmar, Laos, Thailand, Cambodia and Vietnam who live near it. Lush green vegetation and crops line the flat landscape criss-crossed with streams and backwaters.

This page: As the river enters Vietnam it branches into several channels that cover most of the southern lands. The fertile delta extends over Cambodia and Vietnam and is the 'rice bowl' for large areas of both nations, where many different crops and fruits are grown and fish raised. People move around the waterways on boats and many houses are built on stilts to protect them from the ever-present threat of flooding.

Left: My Tho, Can Tho, Chau Doc and Vinh Long are the main towns on the delta and taking a boat ride is an essential tourism activity. My Tho is the main departure point for day-visit tourists to explore the Mekong. These well organized and structured trips enable visitors to see life along the Mekong River and some of the islands in the delta. Visitors can observe agricultural activity, fishing fleets and villages plus take a sampan ride through some of the wetlands.

Below: Near Vinh Long, the Cai Be Floating Market is a colourful morning market, while Cai Rang Floating Market is close to Can Tho. Traders advertise their wares by attaching fruit or vegetables to tall bamboo poles strapped to the masts of their vessels. Others ply the waterways selling prepared meals, such as 'pho' and even serving delicious cups of coffee.

Phu Quoc

The 528-km² (204-sq mile) island of Phu Quoc (Vietnam's largest island) is about the same size as Singapore. It was once a prison but has been transformed to such an extent that it is now perfect for those seeking an isolated island in the sun. There are daily flights from Ho Chi Minh City to the island and ferry services from Ha Tien in the south-west of the Vietnamese mainland near the Cambodian border to Ham Ninh, 100 km (62 miles) away on Phu Quoc's east coast.

This page: Its year-round sunshine, near-deserted beaches and relatively remote location are starting to garner the attention of adventurous tourists. Many consider the beaches here to be the best in Vietnam. They stretch 20 km (12 miles) south from Duong Dong. Visitors not only come to dive and snorkel in the clear waters but also to mountain bike, kayak and trek into the hilly interior peaked by Chua Mountain at 565 m (1,854 ft).

Above: Duong Dong is the principal township situated on the western seaboard. The main resorts, such as the MGallery La Veranda Resort, are located along a 20-km (12$\frac{1}{2}$-mile) stretch of beautiful sands to the south. Watersports, mountain biking and diving in the An Thoi Archipelago to the south are just some of the recreational activities on offer.

Left: In addition to tourism, farming (especially of pepper), fishing and fragrant fish sauce ('nuoc mam') production are important industries. Phu Quoc produces some six million litres (1,560,000 gallons) of premium grade fish sauce and many connoisseurs of 'nuoc mam' argue that the island produces the best in the country.

Getting About

Vietnam is connected to the world via various airlines including the national carrier, Air Vietnam. The main international airports are Hanoi (Noi Bai International Airport), Ho Chi Minh City (Tan Son Nhat International Airport), Danang, Hué, Nha Trang (at Cam Ranh), Phu Quoc, Can Tho and Haiphong while there are another 15 smaller domestic airports. Airports including Hanoi are being enlarged to accommodate the influx of tourists.

Trains are a good way of discovering the main attractions of coastal Vietnam as they stop at all the main cities and towns. One of the world's great train journeys is from Ho Chi Minh City to Hanoi: a 30-hour trip for express trains (and 40 hours for slower ones) of 1,798 km (1,118 miles) on a single track system. Construction on the line started in 1899 and was completed in 1936. Now known as the Reunification Express, several modern trains per day depart in both directions and offer various seating and sleeping arrangements in either hard-class or soft-class. Refreshments are available on the train or from hawkers when the train stops along the way.

Islands, such as Phu Quoc and the marine park of Nha Trang and around Halong Bay, can be reached by boats from the mainland. Travelling along rivers and around the Mekong Delta by boat is another fascinating way to see the country and its people.

As both HCMC and Hanoi grow, negotiating the inner city traffic is something that both fascinates and frightens most visitors. Neither city has a viable public transport system that is suitable for tourists to use, so taxis are the best alternative. Brave visitors will happily jump on the back of motorbike taxis or *xe om*, while others may choose to ride a *cyclo* (a covered trishaw also known as *xich lo*). Cycling is another alternative in the city, while organized bicycle tours of the country are conducted by adventure travel companies.

Resources

Contacts

365travel (Hanoi and HCMC): www.365travelvietnam.com

Asia Travel Guides, Things Asian: www.thingsasian.com

Explorer Tourism Network: www.etn.my

Vietnam Railways: www.vr.com.vn

Vietnam Sea Kayaking Halong Bay with John Gray: www.johngray-seacanoe.com

Vietnam Tourism: www.vietnamtourism.com

References

Bowden, D., Hicks N. and Shippen M. 2013. *Southeast Asia: A Region Revealed*. John Beaufoy Publishing.

Chong, D. 1999. *The Girl in the Picture*. Simon & Schuster.

Fay, K (Editor). 2004. *To Asia with Love: A Connoisseur's Guide to Cambodia*, Laos, Thailand & Vietnam. ThingsAsian Press.

Greene, G. 1955. *The Quiet American*. Penguin Classics Deluxe Edition.

Insight Guides. 2012. *Hanoi & Ho Chi Minh City Smart Guide*. APA Publications.

Lonely Planet Guides. 2013. *Vietnam*.

Films

The 1992 French movie *Indochine* is a good introduction to the variety of landscapes in Vietnam especially around Halong Bay. However, it needs noting that much of this Oscar-winning movie was actually filmed in Malaysia. *The Lover* is another French film filmed around Ho Chi Minh City.

The Graham Greene novel *The Quiet American* is about Greene's life as a news correspondent in French Indo-China during the 1950s. It was made into a movie in 2002.

Other films on Vietnam include: *Green Berets, The Deer Hunter, Apocalypse Now, Born on the Fourth of July, Platoon, Full Metal Jacket* and *Hamburger Hill*.

Acknowledgements

Assistance with photographs was provided by Floyd Cowan, John Arthur and Chad Merchant. Hotel groups such as Accor, Starwood and Angsana are acknowledged for their support. Specific thanks go to Khiet Le, Cynthia Dammerer, Vasu Thirasak and Catherine Racsko. Logistical support was offered by Nguyen Thi Thanh Nga, Le Xuan Hung, Nguyen Thai Quang and Mai Thai Cuong from 365travel and Herman Lim plus Samantha Teo from Explorer Tourism Network.

About the Author

David Bowden is a freelance photojournalist based in Malaysia who specializes in travel and the environment. While Australian, he's been in Asia for longer than he can remember and returns to his home country as a tourist. When he's not travelling the world, he enjoys relaxing with his equally adventurous wife Maria and daughter Zoe. He is also the author of other books in the *Enchanting* series on Borneo, Singapore, Malaysia, Bali & Lombok and Langkawi.

Index

**ASIA
BOOKS**

Published and Distributed in Thailand by Asia Books Co., Ltd.
Bann Jucker House, 14th Floor, 99 Soi Rubia, Sukhumvit 42 Road, Phrakanong, Klongtoey, Bangkok 10110, Thailand
Tel: (66) 2-715-9000; Fax: (66) 2-715-9197; Email: information@asiabooks.com; www.asiabooks.com

First published in the United Kingdom in 2014 by John Beaufoy Publishing,
11 Blenheim Court, 316 Woodstock Road, Oxford OX2 7NS, England
www.johnbeaufoy.com

ISBN 978-1-909612-21-1

Designed by Glyn Bridgewater
Cartography by William Smuts
Project management by Rosemary Wilkinson

All photos by David Bo   ); Floyd Cowan (p40-1,
p43 top and bottom,   t (p64, p65 centre and
bottom); Laguna Lăng C   5 top, p66 top, p68, p69
top); MGallery La Vera   el and Spa (p58 top and
bottom); Shutterstock   centre and bottom, p73

Back cover (left to right   ndara resort at Nha Trang
© Evason Ana Mand   hiet © David Bowden.
Front cover (left to righ   © David Bowden; Hôtel